Push You Away

Maureen

Maureen Anne Meehan

www.maureenannemeehan.com
info@maureenannemeehan.com

Table of Contents

Author's Note

As a sequel to 60 Dates in Six Months (With a Broken Neck), it was my vision to reach out to readers and see what their worst dating experience was. In this quest, we learn that dating can be the depths of hell. People can be cruel, thoughtless, immature, selfish, narcissistic, outrageous, and liars. I was so impressed that readers were willing to share their stories—as difficult as it may have been. I've learned that one must keep their sense of humor intact when dating because you can't just make this stuff up and it is healthier to laugh about it than cry.

Thank you to all readers who've shared this dumpster dive into dating which I equate to "searching for dinner at your local dump." Sounds appetizing, I know!

I received some very encouraging feedback from readers who had terrible experiences who have since found love. It gives us hope that if you stick it out, maybe just maybe you'll be lucky enough to find love! So cheers to holding out hope!

Dedication

Push You Away is dedicated to all readers who have not given up on finding love. This process requires patience and perseverance. Thank you to Writers Branding and Reading Glass Books for the incredible support and guidance throughout this process. It has been my pleasure working with such talent and dedication. I tip my hat in particular to Andrea Morrison who encouraged me to reconsider marketing my legal thrillers in the Mary MacIntosh series and for pondering the idea of writing nonfiction satire. We have had a lot of laughs over this!

Cheers to hope and love. May you always have both.

Maureen

"May the road rise up to greet you
May the wind be always at your back
May the sun shine warm upon your face
May the rain fall soft upon your fields
And until we meet again
May God hold you in the palm of His Hand"

Little Belittle

A successful real estate agent has been seeing a woman for some time. He's a very handsome man and most likely one of the top agents in South Orange County. This woman is a head turner, and she knows it. But she's also not very nice. She just wants to talk about herself (think the Toby Keith song "I Want to Talk About Me"). She doesn't want to know about this man, and anytime he does offer a glimpse of his life, she constantly belittles him and made him feel less than worthy of her love. She was rude to him and to others like waitstaff at restaurants. It was emotionally draining for him over time and so he had to let this stunner go.

She's still around looking as good as ever, and he bumps into her from time to time at local popular places, but he knows better than to reach out again. She's not worth it.

Prego

Unbeknownst to this man, he was dating a woman who was pregnant and in her first trimester. She did not disclose the fact that she was pregnant nor did she disclose the fact that she was also dating the father of her child. This three way went on for months until he started noting changes in her body. When he asked her about it, she had no choice other than to come clean about the pregnancy (but not about the fact that she was still having relations with the baby's father).

One can imagine that he was concerned that he was in fact the father of this unborn child, and when he inquired, she admitted that it was someone else's. But then it dawned on him that if he continued to date her, he was likely going to be stuck raising some other man's child.

It's not that he doesn't like children, but his are adults now and he's not in the market to have more children. He also is unaware that she's still dating the father of the child.

She finally comes clean as the pregnancy progresses. That was the end of that.

How Late is Too Late?

Fashionably late? Punctual? Most people have their own clock and decide when they will make their grand entrance. But some are less considerate of other people's time.

This guy was not very considerate of her time. He was communicative that he was running a tad bit late, but he underestimated himself by a lot.

He was three hours late for dinner. After the third hour, she went home.

Short Arms, Deep Pockets

A very handsome man asks her out to dinner, and they agree to meet at a posh restaurant. They sit down and begin to chat. They have plenty of things in common, and the conversation flows.

They both order an appetizer to share and a nice bottle of Pinot Noir. Each orders an entrée. They eat, and after dinner, it is getting late on a worknight, so they ask for the check.

Then he suddenly declares that he has somehow forgotten his wallet. He feigns embarrassment, and she is stuck with a several-hundred-dollar dinner bill. She has no choice but to pay.

She never hears from him again.

Cats are not Included

Gorgeous fireman is a dating app connection, and he commences the texting marathon. She finally agrees to go for coffee with him at a cool café halfway between where they reside. They are both punctual, and he looks exactly like his photos, so that's good.

They order their coffees and he pays. That's a plus. They sit down outside and begin chatting about the things that they have in common. It's been about an hour of conversation and everything is going smoothly. He's articulate and is talking about his plans for retirement later in the year and how he perceives he will spend his time. He's fully vested in his pension. Another plus.

She's joking that she's never going to be able to retire because she has two cats and one of them is huge and is addicted to cat treats.

His mood suddenly changes. She inquires. He says that he hates cats. Is he allergic? No. Not allergic. Just hates them and won't date anyone who loves cats.

End of date.

Arrogance is Unbecoming on You

It started with a simple friend request on Facebook. His profile showed a handsome man with a charming smile, and his bio indicated that he shared similar interests with her. She was intrigued by him and therefore accepted the friend request.

They hit it off and exchanged messages for hours. He was funny, intelligent, and seemed genuinely interested in getting to know her. After a few weeks of chatting, he asked her out on a date.

Excited and nervous, she agreed to meet him at a cozy café in the city. As she walked in, she immediately recognized him from his profile picture. He looked just as handsome in person and her heart skipped a beat.

But as soon as they started talking, she realized that something was off. He was rude and arrogant and kept making inappropriate statements that made her uncomfortable. She tried to steer the conversation in a different direction, but he kept bringing it back to topics that made her cringe.

As the date went on, she couldn't wait for it to be over. She made up an excuse about needing to leave early and practically ran out of the café. She was so disappointed and frustrated that the guy she had been chatting with turned out to be nothing like she had imagined.

Everything is as it seems on social media. People can portray themselves in a certain way online, but their true colors may only come out in person. From that day on, she decided to only meet men in public places for first dates. And as far as that guy from Facebook? She never spoke to him again.

Hair on Fire!

When I was sitting across the table from him about to whisper something romantic in his ear, my hair caught on fire, and he doused me with his glass of water.

I went to the restroom to clean up, and when I returned to the table at this posh place, he was gone. The bill was not.

All of My Exes Live in . . . This Date

One of the worst dating experiences of my life. I was in college and I finally mustered the courage to ask out my long-term crush. We had been friends for years and I thought there was a mutual connection between us.

I planned a romantic dinner date at a fancy restaurant, and I was so excited to spend one-on-one time with him. However, as soon as we sat down at our table, things took a turn for the worse. He spent the entire evening talking about his ex-girlfriend and how much he missed her. He did not ask me a single question about me or show any interest in me or getting to know me better. I felt like I was just a stand-in for his ex, and it was incredibly awkward and uncomfortable.

To make matters worse, he kept checking his phone and texting throughout the meal, completely ignoring me. I felt so disrespected and unimportant.

By the end of the night, I realized that my crush was not the person I thought he was, and I left the date feeling disappointed and heartbroken. It was a painful lesson in unrequited love and the importance of setting boundaries in relationships.

That was a very sad day of my life. But now I am happy and I have found someone compatible and we both fell in love.

Money Does Not Buy You Happiness

I went on some dating sites with the hope of finding true love. I found this man who was so generous and caring. He offered to give me money in exchange for my commitment to him. I felt very controlled by this offer over time and that is the reason I decided to end the relationship.

But I can't lie. I did enjoy the Louis Vuitton and the Prada and the fancy everythings.

81 is Not The New 61

All dressed up for a romantic evening out with someone you have been chatting with for weeks online. I arrived at the restaurant excited to finally meet in person. But as soon as they walk in, you realize that they have lied about their age and appearance. They are at least a decade older than their profile picture and wearing clothes straight out of the '80s.

You decide to give them the benefit of the doubt and try to make the best of it. But things quickly go downhill when they spend the entire evening talking about their exes, complaining about their job, and bragging about their toenail clipping collection. I'm not lying. Toenail clippings. I want to vomit into my own mouth. To top it off, they have terrible table manners, chewing with their mouth open and slurping their soup loudly.

As the night drags on, you find yourself counting down the minutes until you can make a polite escape. When the bill arrives, they conveniently forget their wallet, leaving you to foot the entire bill for the disastrous evening. You leave the restaurant feeling disappointed, frustrated, and vowing to never trust an online profile again.

Put Me IN, Coach, I'm Ready to Play . . .

Talking to this professional baseball coach for weeks but he's on the road and schedules don't align. And then he's finally at a home game and he sends you tickets. You are the Susan Sarandan of baseball, and you could pass as Bull Durham. You love the sport. Your three sons played, and Cooperstown was real. Your nephews played in high school and college. Your dad knows every statistic from nearly a century.

You are enjoying watching what is a very good game. Tim Stroud just had a homerun and you are thinking that this could be a good post-game "interview" with coach.

You have left the game however because it has become cold and he sends you a note that he's going to need extra time with the team for this or that.

You are cool with that.

And then you go home and listen to music and fall asleep.

You awake to a barrage of texts from the teddy bear coach that everyone loves. These are not nice texts. These are angry texts.

Without going into detail to protect the innocent (me) and the guilty (him), let's just agree that he might be not as much of a teddy bear as the media portrayed.

Soon To Be (not) Yours

Online chatting is overrated and tedious, and it is hard to keep the dudes straight. You receive chats at all hours of the day and night, and it can disrupt your sleep and your wakefulness.

In enters "Soon to Be Yours" who is the bloke who is entirely a smartass. That's not a bad thing if you like a wicked sense of humor. But this idiot is not funny. He's simply dull, and the only thing you have in common is that you like to go camping.

Fit Mispelled

I am a fit guy and I go to the gym six days a week and practice yoga and breathing exercises and keep my body in line with the Lord's Temple. I emphasize the importance of fitness in my profile, and my photos are current and depict my fit life of exercise and healthy eating.

She and I talk online and then on the phone for weeks, and she compliments my body constantly and says that she practices the same discipline that I do on a daily basis.

Her pictures are incredible. She could model for Playboy or Victoria Secret. Please don't judge me for being shallow, but I've tried life with Pollyanna and also with the intellectual, and those didn't work out either, so I thought I would just take a time out and have fun.

She shows up for dinner at a nice place that I have made reservations. She's not "fit." She's "fat."

Simply a misspelling?

Stalker (#1)

They had been dating for some time, but things had become less than savory. They had not had intimate relations, and we were really just pals (with her paying most of the bills).

She gives it a minute to get her head together before getting back out there into the cesspool—cognizant of the devil you do know.

She goes on a first date. It's a hike, and he is on time and nice and handsome. They hike six miles and he's fit and they enjoy a very nice conversation.

He gives her a nice kiss, and they make plans for a future date that weekend.

She leaves and is at a stoplight waiting for a left turn and her phone rings on Bluetooth. It's the Ex. He says to look right. She does. It's him. He's stalking her.

To be continued . . .

Supermodel Stalker

One date with a gorgeous female who looks to be a supermodel. He's new to the dating world after nearly thirty years of marriage.

They go out and she goes home with him. Rookie mistake. She knows where he lives and what he drives.

Fast forward. This lady leaves him voicemails and notes and you name it. He can barely leave the house not knowing where or what she is.

He starts a new relationship with a professional woman. Great lady. This stalker infiltrates her profession, and it ruins any potential with this professional.

It happens again with another professional. Second professional woman is afraid to have this crazy woman in her life. Her job is dealing with unsteady people, and she has professionally seen what this can look like. She sabotages it to avoid what could have been great.

Costco Stalker

She meets him online, and he has a great job with Costco doing the fresh wrap fish process wherein he has a team at the docks who fresh wrap the fish once cleaned and ready for market. This is a big money business with the entire Costco chain all over the USA.

The agreement is to meet in the middle and have dinner at a place he has suggested. In her mind, there were a lot of better places, but she doesn't want to emasculate.

He meets her at her car and brings her a giant bouquet of flowers in a fancy vase. She is grateful but does not want to carry a Waterford vase of flowers into a restaurant, so they buckle the bouquet into the front passenger seat of her SUV and go and have dinner. Conversation flows for a while until he reveals how he spent his day: at the District Attorney's Office getting a restraining order against his stalker.

Fast forward to the end of the evening and he walks her to his car to say goodnight and give her a soft kiss. Unfortunately, they discover that her car has been keyed. Not just a little. A lot.

He knows who did it. The bouquet was a mistake. He offers to pay for her to have her entire car repainted. He feels terrible. She feels terrified and now deceived. He should have told her about the stalker and the DA and the TRO before the date. She would not have agreed to date him.

She gets home and texts him that she is safely home. He is happy to hear from her and wants to VenMo her money for the repairs. And then he sends her a DPick.

She pays for the paint job and blocks him.

Stalker (#1 continued)

Picking up from the freeloader dude.

Stalking incident from the hiking date fresh in her mind, she agrees to meet another guy at a coffee shop in a different town.

She arrives, and he's placed and paid for her coffee. They sit and talk for forty-five minutes and then proceed on a hike. The hike is great and it is several hours before he kisses her goodbye (for now) at her car. She's lucky she didn't get a parking ticket as she didn't expect the date would go two hours longer than it did.

She had left her phone in her car as well as her iPhone earbuds, and her phone was tracking the Waze App as she needed to take her daughter to the airport on an international flight.

She gets in her car and looks at her phone to let her daughter know that she's on her way home to get her for the airport run.

The text from the freeloader says, "I thought you didn't like Starbucks."

Upset, she goes straight to the AT&T store and asks how this dude is tracking her. Two ways: Earbuds. Waze App.

Earbuds go in the Veteran's donation bag. Lord knows where they are now. Waze App is gone. New email.

It's treacherous out there. Be careful.

Play Ball

She connected with a baseball coach for a local MLB team, and they agreed to meet for drinks in Newport Beach upon his return from a road trip to Cincinnati. However, his flight was late, and it was too late to meet. Instead, he invited her to attend the next game locally. He sent her great tickets.

She attended dressed in her garb as she has three sons who played baseball and went to Cooperstown and loved to attend these games as a family. The game was a great one and the team won. However, it was a late game and it gets cold, so she left after the seventh inning stretch.

She went home and had a glass of wine and went to sleep. She awoke to a barrage of angry texts for not staying after the game to hook up. He accused her of not being grateful for the tickets. She had thanked him multiple times for the tickets.

Next at bat.

Winter Girl

She thought everything was going well in their relationship, but then one day she came across a post on social media that shattered her world. It was a picture of her partner with someone else, captioned with heart emojis and declarations of love.

Her heart sank as she realized that her partner had been cheating on her. The betrayal and hurt were indescribable. She couldn't believe that someone she trusted and loved could do something so cruel and deceitful.

She confronted him about the post, and he denied it at first, but when she showed him the evidence, he finally admitted to his infidelity. He apologized and begged for forgiveness, but the damage was done.

She felt humiliated and heartbroken, knowing that her partner had been sharing intimate moments with someone else while pretending to be committed to her. The trust that she had in this man was completely shattered, and she knew that their relationship could never be the same again.

In the end, she had to muster the courage to walk away from the person who had hurt her so deeply. It was a painful and difficult decision, but she knew that she deserved better.

This experience taught her to be more cautious and guarded in future relationships and to always trust her instincts when something doesn't feel right. It was a painful lesson to learn, but one that ultimately made her stronger and more resilient in the face of heartbreak.

Bestie

She once went on a date with a guy who seemed really sweet and charming. They went to a fancy restaurant and he insisted on paying for everything which she thought was really kind of him. However, as the night went on, she noticed that he was paying a lot of attention to her best friend who had joined them for the evening. She brushed it off at first, thinking maybe she was just being paranoid.

But as the night went on, it became more and more obvious that he was more interested in her best friend. He would constantly flirt with her and make inside jokes that she didn't understand. It was incredibly awkward and uncomfortable for her, and she couldn't wait for the date to be over.

To make matters worse, at the end of the night, he asked for her best friend's phone number right in front of her. She was completely humiliated and hurt. It was clear that he had no interest in her at all, and she felt like she had wasted her time and energy on someone who was only interested in her bestie.

It was definitely her worst dating experience, and it taught her to be more cautious and observant when it comes to dating. It also made her realize the importance of surrounding oneself with people who respect and value her.

Ritzy

He asked her to meet him at the Ritz Carlton rooftop bar overlooking the Pacific Ocean for a drink. They would have dinner at a nice restaurant at the Ritz if everything was going well. She felt like that was a fair boundary. He was every bit as handsome as his pictures, and he was well educated, articulate, and had extremely good manners. He greeted her at the door, walked her to a table, and pulled out her chair. He took her handbag and placed it on the chair next to her and assisted in scooting her in.

He handed her the drink menu and the appetizer menu and proceeded to tell her that the ahi stack appetizer was a little spicy but flavorful. They ordered wine and the appetizer, and he held her hand and gazed into her eyes and asked her meaningful questions. They talked with ease and he was funny. He poked fun at himself and didn't take himself too seriously despite his obvious success in business.

After they finished their wine and appetizer, he invited her to dinner at the new restaurant. He again escorted her to the table and assisted her with her jacket and handbag. He handed her a menu and gave her time to look it over.

When the staff approached, he kindly inquired about any specials and asked for recommendations. He accepted the recommendations and, after conferring with her, placed their orders along with a nice bottle of wine.

They enjoyed a fabulous meal together and continued to converse with ease. They laughed often. And then all of the sudden his mood soured. He grew pensive and morose and started talking about his ex-wife with utter disdain. It was like a light switch was flipped. His personality changed. He started yelling at her as if she was the ex-wife who had divorced him. People were staring at them. She grew increasingly more embarrassed and confused by this behavior.

She wanted to go home, and so she politely waived for the check. He swiped it from her and paid the bill with his American Express card. He then calmed down a little. After the bill was processed, they gathered their belongings to leave. And then he asked the waitress for his AmEx card. She indicated that she thought she had returned it with the bill that he signed, but she politely said that she would double-check for him.

The date excused herself to the restroom while they sorted out the credit card. When she returned from the restroom, he was having words with the manager. The staff at the Ritz was searching frantically for the card to no avail. The date asked him if he had checked his wallet. He looked at her as if she had two heads and then reluctantly checked. The AmEx was in his wallet.

The date profusely apologized to the staff and quickly escorted herself to the valet and went home. Alone. That was the end of that.

It's Optional to be Divorced

They had been on several dates starting with a hiking date and then dinner the same day. They hit it off well. He was as handsome as his pictures, and he was well educated and an accomplished professional. He had two adult children who were launched and independent. They agreed to another date, and after dinner, he accompanied her to her home. They put on some music and opened a nice bottle of wine that he had brought. They were conversing on the couch and kissing and enjoying getting to know each other better.

He inquired about her past and her kids and divorce and she was candid. She then reciprocated the line of questioning, and he grew increasingly uncomfortable. She picked up on this and then decided to be more direct in her line of questioning. She asked point blank when his divorce was final. It wasn't. They were separated for two years but not divorced.

She was upset as she had made it perfectly clear that she was disinterested in dating anyone who wasn't divorced. It violated her religion and her ethics.

He was understanding and said goodnight. That was the end of that.

Selfishly Blind

I was excited that a friend set me up on a blind date because it had been a bit of a dry spell. The guy seemed all right at first, but as the night went on, it became painfully clear that he was completely self-absorbed. Throughout dinner, he completely monopolized the conversation, talking endlessly about himself without even bothering to ask me a single question.

What made it so unforgettable was just how oblivious he was. It's one thing to talk about yourself, but to completely ignore your date's interests and feelings? Total disaster.

Unequal Expectations

There is one time that I met this guy who was charming and attractive, and we both agree that it was a casual fling with no strings attached. However as we start spending more time together, I start to develop strong feelings for him. I am hoping that he is starting to feel the same way, but he continues to treat the relationship as purely physical.

As I continue to grow deeper in love, I realize that he is not looking for anything other than a casual relationship. Despite my feelings (that I now conveyed to him), I struggle to accept the reality of the situation. Eventually I have to come to terms with the fact that he will never see me more than a casual hookup.

This experience left me feeling heartbroken and used as I realized that I was hoping for something more meaningful while he was only interested in physical intimacy. It serves as a painful reminder of the importance of setting boundaries and being honest about my intentions in relationships.

Affairs of The Heart

I met a guy in a bar and we hit is off right away. We ended up going back to his place and things quickly escalated to the bedroom. However, my excitement turned to horror when I noticed a wedding ring on his nightstand. I confronted him about it, and he sheepishly admitted that he was married. I felt sick to my stomach, realizing that I had unknowingly become the other woman in a cheating husband's affair.

I was filled with such guilt and shame for being part of such a deceitful situation. I couldn't believe that he had lied to me and betrayed his wife in such a callous manner. I quickly gathered my things and left, feeling disgusted with myself for being involved with someone who was so dishonest and unfaithful.

The experience left me feeling used and betrayed, and it made me question my judgment in men. It was a painful lesson in the importance of honest and integrity in relationships, and I vowed to never again be part of someone else's infidelity.

Nosey Neighbor

My worst dating experience was when I was living with my boyfriend and he ended up cheating on me with my neighbor. It was a complete betrayal of trust and made me question everything about our relationship. I felt humiliated and heartbroken, knowing that he had been sneaking around behind my back with someone who lived just a few doors down. It was a painful reminder that sometimes the people closest to us can hurt us the most.

In the end, I had to pick up the pieces of my shattered heart and move on from the toxic relationship.

Sarcastic Camper

We've talked for a few weeks on the phone after texting a ton and finally exchanged cell phone numbers. She has a sexy voice and is upbeat and I must admit that I couldn't wait for her name to pop up in a text or call. We agree to meet at a new swank restaurant in Newport Beach near Fashion Island. She shows up and she's darling and dressed well and her pictures match her face and figure. I'm already excited because I have had so many dates where they don't look anything like their dating app photos.

I wait for her in the lobby, and she's only a few minutes late but has had the courtesy to text me with her ETA. We get seated across from one another in a booth and we proceed to talk nonstop while agreeing on an appetizer and we each order a drink.

Conversation flows with ease, and we both have adult children and are empty nesters looking to find love again. Which naturally brings us to the next topic. What do we have in common? I have included in my profile a detailed description of things I like to do. Her profile is somewhat sparse in this regard.

I love to go to the beach and the mountains and camping and golfing and skiing, and I am a hopeless romantic and sarcastic as all get out. I think I am funny but maybe not all people get me. I ask her what she does for hobbies, and she says that she likes to work out and go shopping. That's all. Not one matching activity to anything I like. I don't give up easily, so I asked her if she was willing to learn to camp or ski or golf. I am a patient instructor and am happy to teach her to have some activities in common. She says no.

We finish our dinner with a bottle of wine and I pay the bill. I walk her to her car and promise to call her for a second date. But I never do.

Persian Princess

We match on the dating app mainly because she is Persian. I am Persian. She is remarkably beautiful and age appropriate, so after a few days of exchanging texts, we agree to meet for dinner. We live forty-eight miles apart, so I choose a place that is closer to where she lives. We meet and she is punctual at this beautiful restaurant on the beach in Carlsbad. We are seated at a window table overlooking the Pacific Ocean, and everything seems to be going very well. It is getting close to sunset and so we order wine and toast to another beautiful sunset in Southern California.

I am a biotech engineer with a good job after getting my MBA at a good school back East. She's IVY – Princeton with a degree in literature. This is looking better and better. My mom is Persian and an avid reader, and she wants me to marry an educated Persian woman. This woman is perfect in these two categories. However, we have nothing in common. I'm very athletic and spend my free time outdoors doing sports like scuba diving and surfing and snowboarding and hiking. She doesn't like to do anything outdoors. She likes going to the mall.

We had a nice dinner together, and we had an overall enjoyable evening, however with nothing in common, being Persian and smart was not enough. My mom would have liked her though!

Dogs Rule, Cats Drool

We both like to surf and snowboard and so I ask her out to dinner in Huntington Beach near where we both live and love to surf. She shows up at the restaurant and she is cute and fit. We seem to have a lot in common, and we start talking about surfing together over dinner. We also agree that it would be great to go boarding together in Mammoth as they once again have good snow. Everything is going really well, and I'm pretty hopeful that I have met someone who I can do the things I love with.

We continue to converse over dinner, and she mentions that she has two dogs. I love all animals and I grew up with yellow labs, so her having dogs is a plus. I tell her that I have a couple cats as my job doesn't allow me the time that dogs require. You would have thought I said that I like to kill people. She absolutely hates cats. Spawn of the devil are cats. I think she is joking with me, so I sort of laugh with her and then I realize that she's dead serious about her hatred of the felines.

It was a deal breaker for her. I left feeling deflated. She was so cute and we had so much in common, but I can't give up my cats for a gal who only likes dogs.

Trump Lovers Need Not Apply

He and I have so much in common. He's a dentist and I am a pediatrician. He's tall and handsome and is into nutrition and cooking. He loves to surf and snowboard and enjoys concerts and dancing and going to sporting events. We agree to meet for dinner at a place in San Clemente on Del Mar Street. He shows up on time, and we get a nice table away from the loud and busy bar. We order an appetizer and drinks, and we start chatting about our favorite surf breaks and where we enjoy going snowboarding. Everything is going really well. He has nice table manners and allows me to order for myself. It is amazing how many men try to order for you. I'm a fiercely independent woman and well educated and I am capable of ordering what I like.

One of his questions on the dating app was, "Who Would You Want To Have Dinner With?" I answered Reese Witherspoon because I admire her for her tenacity in Hollywood with acting and then her subsequent transition into her book club and her movie production. He finds this choice to be a good one. I return the question to him. His response was Donald Trump. He loves Trump. He's a Trumpster. He doesn't see my perspective on his lack of class and presidential decorum. I can tell that this is not going well at all. We will just need to agree to disagree, and I asked for the check and I paid it. He disagreed with me paying the bill. I didn't care. I wanted to leave and go home and curl up with Reese Witherspoon's latest book club book and read and go to sleep.

Balboa Blues

He's handsome and lives on Balboa Island and owns a boat and loves to golf and he's retired well with a nice home near the water on the island. We agree to go for a hike in the Back Bay of Newport Beach, and he says that he'll bring charcuterie and wine for a beach picnic after our hike. That sounds nice.

He ends up running late that day with some errands that he needed to accomplish, so he asks that I instead meet him at his house on the island and we can take his dog for a walk around Balboa. That also sounds nice. He sends me his address, and I drive a mile to the coast and park and walk to his house. We grab his dog and walk and talk and enjoy each other a lot. However, he looks old! He's not that old and he has the most stunning ice-blue eyes, but he's weathered. Too much time on the water and the golf course and he looks seventy-five, not sixty-five.

We enjoyed the picnic on his porch with his dog. But I drove home disappointed that he didn't take better care of his health. He was also rather overweight.

Play Me Some Country Music

I match with this cute gal from Irvine and I live nearby, so that's good. We both went to UCSB, but she's a few years older than me, so we didn't meet on campus. I have a wicked sense of humor despite being a CPA and she seems to laugh at my jokes. I'm trying to see if we have much in common during our phone conversation, and she says that she likes to go to concerts and sporting events. That's enough for me, so I ask her if she wants to meet for dinner at a place near her place by the Spectrum mall. She agrees.

She shows up dressed in leggings and an oversized top and it is clear that she's overweight. Her face is cute, but she's a big gal. We proceed to get seated and order drinks, and I'm trying my best with icebreaker jokes to make her at ease. I know that it is not going to work out. But I haven't had many hits lately on the app, so at least I'm not home alone on a Friday night watching TV.

We have a nice conversation about baseball which we both enjoy and I tell her about my favorite baseball move of Bull Durham. She likes it as well. And then we talk about concerts. There are a lot of free summer concerts in Orange County, and they are fun to go to and dance. She said that she loves to do that. She doesn't golf or ski, but she likes to go to concerts and dance, so there's a start. I ask her about what kind of music that she likes. Acid rock. I like all types of music such as rock, country rock, country, reggae, jazz, etc., but I don't like acid rock.

I knew that this wasn't going anywhere before acid rock, but that sealed the deal.

Melbourne Bound

We have been texting for weeks quite frequently but at odd hours for me and he's confident and healthy and loves to travel and ski and seems worldly. We talk about traveling together and places that are on our bucket list, and our list aligns nicely. I asked him where he skis mostly and he said the Remarkables. I clarified New Zealand? Near Queenstown? Yes. I then asked him where he lived. Melbourne. Talk about geographically undesirable.

Opposites Attract, or Do They?

I am an electrical engineer and love to camp, snowboard, go boating, surfing, mountain biking, and hiking. I spend my days indoor working, but the minute the working day is done, I'm at the gym or in the water or on the trail. Sometimes all of the above.

I match with this gal who is exceptionally cute but a little younger than what I date. I'm fifty, and she's in her thirties. My kids are aging out and heading to college soon, and we have not discussed that yet. We meet near a beach and have lunch. It was fun. She's very cute and bubbly and fit.

I start telling her about my upcoming weekend plans which include some of the sports that I like. She says that she's going to a speed puzzle event in Los Angeles. I had never heard of speed puzzle, so I asked her. It's when groups of people who love to do puzzles meet at a convention and compete as to who can finish a hard puzzle fast. It is all weekend. Indoors.

I know that we don't have much in common, so we end lunch and we never correspond again.

Kids!

I meet this lady for dinner in Newport Beach and she's attractive and young. I have told her on the phone that I am the director of sales at a major environmental company and that my job is stressful and requires travel. But when I'm home, I love concerts and sports and music. I live alone in a house that I own and I have a dog who isn't supposed to sleep in the bed but sneaks in every night. She's kind of humored by this.

I ask her about the things she likes to do, and she responds that she loves her job as a pharmaceutical rep for a skin care line. She has great skin, so I am not surprised by her trade. She lives in an apartment nearby and she is geographically desirable. I tell her about my kids as all three are great adults and moving forward with their lives post college.

She then springs it on me. She has no kids but wants them. She's hinting strongly that she wants kids with me. I explain that I had a vasectomy promptly after my third kid.

That was the end of that.

Saddle Up

He's a handsome man aged fifty-eight, and he is a paramedic and tall. He loves the beach and music and beer and travel and has a dog. He also has a horse, and he describes the horse as the love of his life. He asks if I like horses and I say yes but that I don't have much experience riding them. He wants a lady who has a horse. I don't.

The end.

Bored Out Of My Gourd

He has a good job as the director of sales at a pharmaceutical company and he's tall, dark, and handsome. He likes golf and music and cooking and has an MBA from a good school and loves country music. He seems great on paper.

I'm a nurse and work at a local hospital and have earned the status to work the shifts I want to work which has allowed me to take care of my two kids who are now in college.

We agree to exchange telephone numbers and proceed to schedule a time in the evening to talk. Within minutes of answering his call, I am bored to tears. He has a monotone voice and no hobbies and few friends or family. He mainly watched TV.

I'm active and engaged and have a lot of friends and family and love to get out and do things like sporting events and concerts and working out. It's just not going to work out.

Sprouting A Shoplifter

I consider myself a fairly normal guy at age sixty-five as CEO of my company. I like to go for hikes, skiing, concerts, cooking, and I like college football (UCLA Bruins despite a bad season 2023–2024). My next bucket list trip is to Kenya and Tanzania to watch the wildebeest migration, and I love to travel in style and can afford to do so.

I am matched with this darling lady who is age appropriate and has kept herself in good shape for her age. We text and talk for a few weeks and then decide it is date time. She comes to my house for the first date (which I thought was pretty gutsy), and she is early. I need to go to Sprouts for our appetizer and then the plan is dinner out. She jumps in my car and we head to Sprouts together and that's when things go south. She starts eating candy out of the bin, and then she wants me to emulate her dead husband. Making matters worse, she starts crying at dinner, and her mascara is running down her cheeks and people are staring at me like I'm the ass that is breaking up with her at dinner!

I'm so embarrassed. It is our first date! People are looking at me like I am the villain set out to break up a long-time relationship. This experience taught me to talk more on the phone and ask better questions like, how do you feel about being a young widow, and what is your pet peeve?

I've since found a few normal ladies to date, but I have not found "the one" yet.

My Place Or Mine?

I have been dating this guy for a few months, and things have been going exceptionally well. We text every morning from our respective beds and Facetime at night from bed and rendezvous often for a quickie or a quick kiss or lunch or dinner. We see each other often but mostly during the day. It never dawns on me that we don't go out much in the evening. Perhaps it is because we are in constant contact and do communicate with high frequency. We are both busy professionals, and he claims that he has client dinners often at night, so it is understandable. I tend to do client lunches and hustle back to the office.

He's sixty-four and the director of operations at a Fortune 500 company and is humorous, passionate, successful, fit, attractive, and adventurous. He loves concerts and festivals, but also loves to stay at home and bake bread. He's complex and a sharp dresser, but also not afraid to roll up his sleeves and do yardwork. Weird thing is that I've never been invited to his house. He always comes to my house or we meet at restaurants, etc. Over time though I ask if we can go to his place and not mine, but he consistently comes up with an excuse. It becomes annoying to me, so I google his address and decide to go to his house to make sure he's not a fraud.

I show up at his house, and there is a lady there doing the gardening. She is not dressed like a gardener. She's dressed like a housewife. The garage is open and her car is there (along with his) and she has a nice SUV with personalized plates. She has gloves on, so I can't see if she's sporting a ring but I suspect that she is. I want to get out and introduce myself as her husband's mistress, but she looks too nice. She looks like a person that I would be friends with. She doesn't deserve what I'm about to serve.

I call him and he answers (because his wife is outside gardening). I text him a picture that I just took from my car in front of his house and ask him if he knows the lady messing with his flowers. He immediately freaks out on me and accuses me of being a stalker. I have been sleeping with this man on a regular basis for four months and he's now yelling at me for investigating the questions that I have regarding the nature of our relationship.

I allow him the opportunity to play the blame game. It's all my fault. Narcissist. I learned a valuable lesson about following my gut and asking the questions in my head.

DNA, Anyone?

He seemed like a normal guy at age sixty-seven as a retired real estate developer who was handsome and fit and loved to travel. He loves music and concerts and dancing and good wine.

I'm a professional woman and I like a successful businessman and I consider myself attractive and fit and well-read and well-traveled. I'm not a prude by any means, but I'm not frivolous with my body, and I'm not having relations unless it is with someone with whom I share feelings.

We meet for dinner after work one evening on a Thursday and we agree to meet halfway as we live sixty-seven miles apart. It is a reasonable choice, but we both need to work on Friday, so we agree that we will need to call it by nine to get home in time for a quick chat and a good night over the phone kiss. Like I said, he seems normal.

Our next date is set for Saturday night, and he agrees to drive my way to have dinner at a posh restaurant near my home. We go out and have a marvelous time, so I invite him to my home for a nightcap. Big mistake.

He's into kinky slinky and he is Billy Bob Thornton Angelina Foley I want a vile of your blood around my neck before I throw knives at you blindfolded in your bedroom before I have sex with you.

I excuse myself to the restroom and grab my mace and my phone and tell him to get out of my house. Weirdo.

Faith

She seems great. She is attractive and employed and not looking to be saved and her kids aren't leeches. I'm a successful retired financial guy who made it by himself by working godless hours on the Wall Street floor. I'm healthy and the ladies tell me that I am handsome. I go to the gym six days a week and my health is important.

She mirrors some of this for sure, but as we get deeper into core conversation about what we are looking for, one of my commandments is that you must have a strong faith in our Savior. I don't particularly care about your faith in that it can be of variety, but I want you to have a higher Being in your life. I do and it is a cornerstone.

This conversation ends poorly. She's an atheist. Game over.

9-1-1

She met this man on a dating app, and he said that he was very fit and did bike racing and went to the gym frequently. She is very into fitness, so it was crucial to her that anyone she dates be physically active and in decent shape. She doesn't have unreasonable expectations and the guy doesn't need to have a six-pack, but she also doesn't want to date a man with a giant beer belly and fleshy legs.

They agree to meet in Santa Monica near the Pier, and they are planning to go on a hike. There are a few good ones around, and once they meet, they plan to lace up our shoes and go. It is a nice spring day, and they agree to dress casual in hiking clothes and then bring a change of clothing in the event they want to grab a bite to eat thereafter.

She is fifty-two and has been divorced for a few years and has gone on a lot of dates. She considers herself attractive and fit and she has no problems getting dates. The problem is whether the person that she is matched with looks like their photos or is "fit" and not "fat." This gentleman looks like his photos, and he looks to be in decent hiking shape. He has what she thought were "biking legs."

They take off on this hike, and he seems to be keeping up at first, but as she starts the climb, he is falling back a tad and needs to take frequent breaks for water. During one of the breaks, she notices that he looks clammy. She asks if he is okay, and he says he is, but all of a sudden, he collapses. She calls 9-1-1.

He had a heart attack.

Bohemian Renaissance Autodidact Caveman

It caught her attention on the dating app so much so that she had to look up a word. She's an educated woman who teaches third grade, so it is unusual for her to not know the definition of a word.

They had exchanged texts for a few weeks and had agreed to meet for coffee on a Saturday mid morning. They worked out the details of the coffee date and had confirmed the day before. He was a retired fireman and was a good-looking man with a good pension and time off. He took early retirement because he was injured on the job and needed to have knee surgery. He was recovered at this point.

The coffee date went well and conversation flowed. They agreed that they should meet for dinner the following evening. She was very much looking forward to it. The conversation didn't address his app title, but she wanted to ask him about it over dinner the next day.

She went back to the app later that evening to remind herself what his opening line was on the app. It read: "Bohemian Renaissance Aesthete Gentleman Caveman. Autoditact. Healthy. Libidinous. Sapiosexual. Verile. Father. Writer. Poet. Sculptor. Designer. Woodworker. Sailor. Pilot . . . you know. I am looking for a lover, partner, and friend; a profound connection with a woman of character and substance."

This seemed incongruent with the retired fireman that she just had coffee with. She decided that it would be a good opening conversation at dinner the next day.

They met at an agreed-upon restaurant, and they were both punctual. She was dressed in jeans and a sweater with booties, and he was wearing jeans with a button-down shirt and fashionable shoes. He looked nice. He was bald in a good way. She likes bald men with piercing blue eyes, which was exactly what this guy had.

They were seated, and they ordered drinks and an appetizer, and while they waited for these to show up, she asked him about his opening paragraph in his app. He flushed a bit. She told him that the words didn't sound like words that a retired fireman would use. He seemed a little tongue tied. Luckily for him, his beer arrived, and he took a long pull. He set the glass down and said that he needed to tell her something.

It turned out that he did not write his opening for the app. His brother's wife wrote it for him because he didn't know what to write and she wanted to have a little fun with it. It was her opinion that the catchier and flashier, the better. He admitted that he didn't even know what half of the words meant.

They spend half of dinner laughing over the paragraph and deciphering what it meant. They had a great date, and he walked her to the car and gave her a nice appropriate first-date kiss.

She texted him that she made it home safely and all was well.

The end. She never heard from him again. She thought that was poetically Bohemian.

Gentlemen, Rev Your Motors

He is a rare bread at Havasu with his speed boat around guys who want to drive fast. She is there with her parents and siblings and kids and they grew up on the river. They have a family home here, and it has been in their family for generations.

Their family has a ski boat, four jet skis, and all the toys. The kids all know how to drive a truck towing a boat and can back a trailer towing a boat anywhere and can haul a boat out of the water.

This guy drives his cigar boat like a maniac over to their camp one day and he and his useless crew want a pull of his skiers. The cigar boat is too fast to ski behind.

He is handsome. But she is with her family. Her father and mother are on the family boat giving her the stink eye for even engaging in his shenanigans of flirting.

This is a dead end. Permission to board is denied.

Shut The Heck Up

She agreed to meet him for dinner at a nice restaurant near the UCLA campus. He seemed nice enough. Both retired CEOs of Fortune 500 families in Beverly Hills and neither needed the other for anything other than companionship in their seventies.

They both loved to travel and could afford to do it in high style. They have been talking about their next trips, and they agree that if the date goes well, they will merge both of their next trips.

He looks okay—aging not so gracefully. She is put together in her St. John Knit suit for dinner.

The minute they are seated, he starts talking and he never shuts up. One run-on sentence after another talking fast and is the most boring person about how rich he is and how successful he is blah blah blah.

No Bon Voyage.

Collegiate Colleagues

College is supposed to be the time of one's life, and it normally is unless it is not.

He is attending a very liberal school against his wishes because it is one of the best public schools in California. He'd rather not be there, but he has a large academic scholarship as a National Merit Scholar.

The women are all extreme liberals. He is conservative, so he is stifled in conservation and experience.

He decides that he needs to go off campus to possibly meet anyone that is not in the Bay Area of filth and extreme values that don't align.

He is matched with a girl who grew up in this Hell and hates it as much as he does, and they agree to meet for a hike at a nearby botanical garden.

He comes from a large affectionate family, and when they meet at a public place, he goes in for a hug. She does have this sort of a large family and rebukes his affection and goes as far as calling him a CAD. Hilarious.

They enjoy the walk and then agree on dinner which he happily pays for with his part-time job.

Dinner turns into dating for life and marriage.

They are hoping to have a large family.

He's not a CAD after all.

New York Or Bust

It is one thing to be a Persian woman at a liberal college in California when your parents need to know everything about you and who you date or live with or what you eat, but it is a whole new ordeal when you tell them post grad that you are not going to date your Persian guy anymore and you are taking a job in New York City and plan to live alone and start anew.

This is not a love story or a dating story. It is just a fresh start. Be brave. Believe in yourself. It is okay to be alone.

Ozempic Blues

Overweight at twenty-eight in New York City makes it hard to date, and top it off that your female roomies are all skinny Bs.

It's fun to go out in NYC because it is easy to blend in, but the guys ultimately leave the clubs with her roomies and you get to listen to their "music" all night and then she gets to hear them making breakfast with her eggs in the morning when she hides out in her room until everyone leaves.

She learns of a new diet craze called Ozempic, and she meets with a female doctor who gives her a weekly injection. She loses sixteen pounds in a month but feels absolutely terrible and can't stop vomiting, and her intestinal tract is a constant mess and therefore she can't even join her friends out because she is chained to the one-bedroom apartment that she shares with her two roommates in the Village.

Her college friends call and invite her to a party of the coast on a boat. She is excited because she has now lost over twenty pounds and is looking forward to showing up thin. However, her intestinal problems have not subsided.

They are staying at a friend's parents' home on Long Island, and luckily, she will have a bedroom and bathroom to herself. She is usually the life of the party, but these injections are making her feel terrible. She claims that she has a work deadline and holes up in the bedroom because she feels miserable. The weight continues to drop but not without a price.

She still has not gone out on a date because she does not feel like she can even keep a meal down or go dancing. She can't consume alcohol because she is eternally nauseated.

She has to attend a mandatory work meeting in Manhattan, and she avoids the weekly shot so that she is able to take the subway to headquarters. She is starting to feel a little better.

She walks into the conference room and finds her usual place at the large table. She is rifling through the binder as she is behind on work. Her colleague of three years takes his seat next to her. She doesn't notice.

He notices her.

After the meeting which is more of an announcement of future layoffs and corporate downsizing, he asks if she would like to skip out and grab a bagel and coffee. It sounds great, but she doesn't know if she can handle it. She agrees nevertheless.

They place their orders and sit and chat. He is very complimentary and encouraging about her new physical style but explains that he misses her. He expresses that she hasn't been herself for months and that he fell in love with her jovial self. She is shocked by this revelation. He's never shown an interest in her to her knowledge.

He explains that he is shy and that it is not his strong suit to ask a woman out, but that in their work crowd, it was easy to hang with her. Now that she rarely attends anything, he rarely sees her and he misses her a lot.

A bagel and coffee turns into dinner which turns into pillow talk. Her first.

Their first.

Their forever.

Textathon

She once went on a date with a guy who seemed really interested in getting to know her at first. However, as the date went on, he kept checking his phone, and he seemed more in texting his friends than talking to her.

She realized that he was not committed to get to know her and was just looking for someone to pass the time with until he met someone that he was truly interested in. It was disappointing and frustrating, and it made her realize the importance of finding someone who is truly interested in building a connection.

Scandalous Affairs

She never thought that she would find herself in this situation, but here she was caught in the middle of a scandalous affair with her husband's best friend.

It started innocently enough in that they had been married for five years, but things were beginning to feel stale. We were both caught up in our careers and we barely made time for each other. That is when she started spending time with her husband's best friend.

His best friend was charming and attentive, and he made her feel alive in ways that she hadn't felt in years. They started meeting up for drinks and long conversations, and before they knew it, they were sneaking around behind her husband's back.

She felt guilty about what they were doing, but she couldn't help herself. The passion and excitement of the affair was intoxicating, and she found herself drawn to his best friend in a way that she had never felt for her husband.

But as the affair continued, the guilt started to weigh heavily on her, and it was causing her increasing anxiety. She knew that she was betraying her husband in the worst possible way, and she couldn't shake the feeling that she was destroying her marriage.

Eventually her husband found out about the affair. He was devastated and she was left to face the consequences of her actions. She had betrayed the man she had promised to love and cherish, and she had hurt him in the worst possible way.

In the end, her marriage fell apart, and she was left alone with nothing but guilt and regret. She had lost the love of her life and destroyed a friendship in the process. She had cheated on her husband with his best friend, and was left to pick up the pieces of the mess that she had created.

Hawaii Blues

He met a girl while on vacation in Hawaii. She was beautiful and charming and seemed like a perfect match for him. They spent a few days exploring the island together, trying new foods and enjoying beautiful beaches.

But as the days went on, he started noticing red flags. She was constantly on her phone, texting and calling someone he didn't know. She would often disappear for hours at a time leaving him alone wondering where she was and what she was doing.

One night they went for a fancy dinner, and she seemed disinterested and distant. He tried to engage her in conversation, but she was far more focused on her phone that she was on him. He finally confronted her about her behavior, and she admitted that she had been talking with her ex-boyfriend the whole time that they were on vacation.

He was devastated. He had invested time and energy into this relationship, only to find out that she was still hung up on her ex. He realized that he was just a rebound for her and that she was never going to be truly interested in him.

He ended things with her that night and spent the rest of the vacation trying to enjoy himself without her. It was a tough lesson to learn, but he knew that he deserved someone who would give him their full attention and affection. And he vowed to never be taken advantage of like that again.

Doctor Stalker

He was dating a surgeon for about nine months when his ex somehow found out. The ex was a one-night stand and was a little off her rocker and what some might call a Plastic Fantastic in Orange County, California.

The ex started stalking the new love interest and went so far as to make an appointment with the female physician to get to know more about her. The stalker then started calling her office constantly and instant messaging her.

The stalker then started giving the doctor horrible reviews on Yelp and other websites and causing mayhem and havoc in her professional life. It was extremely distressing to the doctor and her staff as she saw more cancellations than appointments.

This behavior resulted in the doctor obtaining a restraining order against the stalker. But that's not where this ends.

The doctor ends the relationship with her boyfriend as a result of this mess, but the now ex-boyfriend continues to communicate with both of them. He knows that he shouldn't, but somehow he is insecure enough to keep this up unfortunately.

Lawyer Stalker

They broke up after he put zero effort into the relationship. She got tired of his lack of initiation and lack of independent thought.

She was busy in her practice and her life with family, friends, and associates. He was busy occupying space. She was a pruner, constantly donating her belongings and cleaning her home. She did all of the shopping and cooking and most of the cleaning and all of the entertaining. He added nothing to her life.

She broke it off after tolerating it for far too long. He was devastated. She was disappointed that he put no effort into the relationship.

She decided after some time to get back out there, and she joined a dating app and went on her first few dates. He showed up each time. She checked her car to see if a tracking device was somehow attached to her vehicle. Sure enough. Apple Tag.

High School Sweetheart

He is a senior in high school and he is very attracted to another senior girl, but they are just in the friend zone despite the fact that he is head over heels with her. He was not even expecting that they would be friends because she was popular and he is not.

A mutual friend invited both of them to a party after a high school event. She was unexpectantly outgoing toward him and very friendly, but the catch is that she has a boyfriend. Once he realized this, he didn't take any shots as he didn't want to get beat up by this jock. He decided that it was enough to be included in her friend zone.

She invited him anytime she went to an event or party and then there was a group trip after graduation and she included both her boyfriend and him on the trip.

She was constantly having arguments with her boyfriend, and within minutes of these fights, she would reach out to her friend for company and to cry on his shoulder.

They continued to pal around at these parties, but one night after she had too much to drink at a party, she accompanied him to his house. He told her that she could sleep in his bed and that he could sleep on the couch. She would not have it and asked that he sleep next to her and hold her for the night. He did but with one eye open, worried that the boyfriend would show up at any time.

The next trip for the seniors was upon then and there was again a lot of drinking involved. He had a hotel room, and she asked to spend the night in his room. There were two beds, so he offered her one of them. She made a pass at him and tried to get him going, but again the boyfriend was still in the picture and he was afraid of him. He opted not to sleep with her as a result despite his hormonal drive.

They never did get physical together due to his respect for her and his respect for his own safety, but it was a disaster for his heart. They remain in the friend zone and he considers her amazing still.

Double Trouble

He met her at a nice restaurant on Newport Coast for dinner. She looked exactly like her photos on the dating app. Perhaps she was even better looking. They enjoy a nice meal with great conversation and she is a delight. They share two entrees and a bottle of wine, and both decline to have dessert.

It is time to wrap it up, and she asks him to join her for a nightcap at the bar. He happily accepts. They order and she wants to sit next to a handsome guy who has been there all night. He's noticed that this guy has been watching them. He doesn't think anything of it. He figures that this guy is in awe of her beauty.

She proceeds to introduce him to the guy at the bar. They know each other. In fact, he is her boyfriend, and they would like to have a threesome. He's utterly floored by this suggestion. He's never had sex with another man and has no desire to do so. He tries to clarify the request, but this couple confirms their desire. He pays for the drinks and leaves, and he never hears from her again.

Smelly Grandma

He meets this woman at a swank new restaurant in Fashion Island in Newport Beach, and they have agreed to meet at the bar for a drink. He arrives on time and texts her. She responds that she is already at the bar and describes what she is wearing. He spots her and proceeds to the stool next to her that she has saved for him.

She looks nothing like her photos. She is fifteen years older and fifteen pounds heavier, and she smells like mothballs and cigarettes. He's mortified.

He orders a stiff drink and they talk for a bit, but within fifteen minutes, he makes up an excuse about his friend who needs help and leaves. He blocks her and never hears from her again.

Bankrupt Bob

They are supposed to meet at a nice restaurant in Laguna Beach on a certain date at a certain time. They have confirmed it. But one hour before the meeting, he texts her and says that he's having car troubles and wants her to pick him up for dinner.

The problems is that he lives about thirty minutes away and it is rush-hour traffic. She's flexible and he's handsome, and so she drives to his apartment complex and texts him that she is outside waiting.

He comes out and he is dressed in a peculiar outfit that looks like something one would throw together at a thrift store. She tries to not be too judgy and he hops in. They drive to Laguna and have dinner, but he's forgotten his wallet at home, and so she has to pay the bill.

On the way to the car, he wants to get a sample of chocolate at a nice chocolatier and so they go in. He decides that he'd like a box of expensive chocolates and he doesn't have his wallet. She pays. She doesn't want any chocolate, but he doesn't offer her any.

She proceeds to drive him home, and she drops him off at the complex. He leans in for a kiss but she passes. He gets out of her car and walks up the steps.

She speeds away and never hears from him again. Good riddance.

Let's Talk About Me

They meet for dinner and a nice place in Newport Beach after texting and talking for a few weeks. He is a handsome man in his mid-sixties and divorced without kids. She is an attractive woman in her late fifties, and they both have managed to stay fit.

They are both dressed nicely as the restaurant is upscale. He has been seated and is waiting for her as she is running a little late. The minute that she arrives, he pops up and greets her with a soft kiss on the cheek and walks her to their table.

They order some wine and an appetizer and start with the small talk. He tells her everything about his life, rarely coming up for air. When he does inquire about something in her life, he talks over her and tells her what he supposedly believes should be her answer. Forty-five minutes have elapsed since they first meet and she's rarely been allowed to speak for herself.

Dinner can't arrive fast enough, and as they finish, she excuses herself to the restroom. She texts a friend and tells her that this date is a nightmare and the friend knows to text her in a minute at the table with an emergency. This will be her emergency escape hatch.

She leaves under the pretense of this emergency, and she never looks back.

Sapiosexual Architect

She is matched with him for their desire to meet someone intelligent who is a professional. There is no doubt that he is both. He's an architect and a lawyer and is well read and has traveled the world. He is into cooking as well, so they have a lot in common.

They meet for a drink and easily chat. She is also a lawyer, and he knows a lot about the law but also about building codes and zoning due to his career in architecture. She is an elder abuse defense attorney, so their areas of law are very different, but that keeps the conversation lively and interesting.

They share their favorite things to cook, and they share the places they have traveled, so conversation continues to flow easily.

However, he has used one word over and over and that is "sapiosexual." She thinks she knows what it means but is not one hundred percent sure, so she asks for clarification. He seems a little put off by her ignorance and responds in a slightly condescending manner that it means a person who is attracted to highly intelligent people. That was what she thought, but she didn't want to make an assumption and be incorrect.

As they order another drink, she continues to notice that he's talking down to her, as if she's not quite keeping up with his pace of intellect. That is not impressive in that she's well accomplished.

And there it is again: "sapiosexual."

She decides to not order another drink and she leaves. This was not her guy.

STD Guy

She's a CPA and has been divorced for years and has not done much dating after going through a messy protracted divorce. She gets matched with a handsome bald man who loves to eat steak. They meet at a nice steakhouse nearby and he brings a nice bottle of wine to share.

She is nervous as she hasn't gone on too many dates. He notices and tells her that it is going to be fine and that she can set the pace.

They start talking and he reveals that he's dated quite a bit for the past five years. He mentions the number of women he's dated and she's growing increasingly concerned about how many people he's been intimate with.

She's a straightforward person, and so she asks him point blank about safety and sexual contact. He is quiet for a beat and then admits that he has an STD but that it's been dormant for a bit. Herpes? Yes, herpes.

Hard pass.

Stagecoach

They are supposed to meet for coffee the Monday after Stagecoach, but he sends her a text message indicating that he is too hung over from Stagecoach and that he needs to go to Las Vegas to recover. She thinks that is an odd way to recover from a hangover, but so be it. To each their own.

He's in Vegas and calls her and says that he is still under the weather because he hooked up with two gals at once and that they worked him over pretty well. He would need additional recovery time.

She passes. Grow up, dude.

College Daze

He was set up on a blind date in college. He attended the University of Wyoming, and she attended the rival Colorado State University. Cowboy vs. Ram. Betting on the Cowboy here.

He and his roommate took the roomie's Mustang to Fort Collins. She drives a two-wheel-drive Chevy Blazer. Being a Wyoming guy, he had no clue that a two-wheel-drive vehicle existed.

They met at some bar and had beer and burgers and decided that it would be fun to drive to Horsetooth Reservoir near campus. They hopped in her Blazer, and he drove the three of them to the "beach." Lo and behold, they got stuck in the two-wheel-drive on the beach. They tried for hours to get this Blazer unstuck to no avail. She didn't equip her car with tools of any nature.

They knew that they would need to walk on the highway back, as now it is dark and near midnight. They had to hitchhike back to his roommate's Mustang and drive back to Laramie, Wyoming, to get his four-wheel drive Dodge pickup truck. He and his roommate drove back to Fort Collins and towed her Blazer off the beach and they drove it to her dorm. It was now the wee hours in the morning. She didn't seem that appreciative.

Money Can't Buy Love

When she matched with a wealthy older man on a dating app, he seemed charming, sophisticated, and successful, and she therefore decided to give him a chance.

Their first date was at a fancy restaurant, and he showered her with expensive gifts and compliments. She was flattered at first, but things quickly took a turn for the worse.

As they continued to see each other, she realized that his family was not on board with their relationship. They made it crystal clear that they did not approve of her—a younger woman—as their father's companion.

Despite his attempts to reassure her that he would stand up to his family, it became increasingly clear that their opinion held more weight than her feelings. He started to distance himself from her, making excuses for why they couldn't see each other as often.

She felt used and disposable, like she was just a temporary distraction for him. It was a painful realization that his wealth and status were more important to him than their connection.

In the end, she had to walk away from the relationship, feeling hurt and disillusioned. It was a harsh reminder that money can't buy happiness or love and that sometimes the worst dating experiences come from those who seem too good to be true.

Love Can Be A Double-Edged Sword

It all started when he met her at a friend's party. She was beautiful, funny, and they hit it off right away. They went on a few dates and he couldn't believe his luck—she was perfect in every way.

But then one day she told him that she had an identical twin sister. He was a bit surprised, but he didn't think much of it at first. That is, until the twin started showing up everywhere they went.

At first he thought it was just a coincidence. But then he started to notice that the twin was always trying to one-up his girlfriend—whether it was with her outfit, her jokes, or even the way she flirted with him.

Things came to a head one night when he had planned a romantic dinner with his girlfriend. The twin showed up unannounced and started flirting with him in front of her sister.

His girlfriend was visibly upset, and he felt caught in the middle of a bizarre love triangle.

He tried to talk with his girlfriend about it, but she was too hurt and confused to listen. In the end, he had to break things off with both of them because he couldn't handle the drama and the constant competition between the twins.

It was a messy and heart-wrenching experience that left him feeling used and manipulated. He learned the hard way that sometimes love can be a double-edged sword, especially when it comes in the form of identical twins!